Know It All!
Beginner Guides to the Big World

Let's Learn All About
Going to School!

WINDMILL BOOKS

Find some fun ways to get to know your numbers on page 46.

Published in 2025 by Windmill Books,
an Imprint of Rosen Publishing
2544 Clinton St.
Buffalo, NY 14224

Copyright © Miles Kelly Publishing Ltd 2023

All rights reserved.

No part of this book may be reproduced in any form without permission in writing from the publisher, except by a reviewer.

Publishing Director Belinda Gallagher
Creative Director Jo Cowan
Editorial Director Rosie Neave
Senior Editor Becky Miles
Managing Designer Joe Jones
Image Manager Liberty Newton
Production Elizabeth Collins
Reprographics Stephan Davis, Venita Kidwai
Assets Lorraine King
Consultant Emma Renard

Cataloging-in-Publication Data

Names: Veitch, Catherine, author. | Busby, Ailie, illustrator.
Title: Let's learn all about going to school! / by Catherine Veitch, illustrated by Ailie Busby.
Description: Buffalo, New York : Windmill Books, 2025. | Series: Know it all!: beginner guides to the big world
Identifiers: ISBN 9781538395981 (pbk.) | ISBN 9781538395998 (library bound) | ISBN 9781538396001 (ebook)
Subjects: LCSH: Schools--Juvenile literature. | Education--Juvenile literature. | School day--Juvenile literature.
Classification: LCC LB1556.V42 2025 | DDC 371--dc23

Printed in the United States of America
CPSIA Compliance Information: Batch #CSWM25: For Further Information contact Rosen Publishing at 1-800-237-9932

Find us on

See everyone arriving at school for their first day on page 12.

It can be good to wind down after school – learn how on page 35.

Know It All!
Beginner Guides to the Big World

Let's Learn All About
Going to School!

Catherine Veitch

Illustrated by Ailie Busby

Contents

- 6   Big school
- 8   Getting ready

- 10   On the way
- 12   The first day
- 14   In the classroom

- 16   Our schedule
- 18   Settling in

I'm so excited about all the books we can read at the library!

- 20   Outside
- 22   Our values
- 24   Around the school

We can discover things outdoors, as well as in the classroom.

26 Making friends
28 Lunchtime
30 What will we learn?

32 The end of the day
34 After school

36 The first week
38 Get moving
40 In the hall
42 Forest school

Nathan has just learned to ride his bike, and loves to ride to school.

44 Wonderful writing
46 Nifty numbers

48 Can you find?

Big school

Miss Smiley has a new class starting school soon. The children have been getting ready by practicing some helpful things at home and talking about what school might be like.

There will be lots of new things to try.

Jasmine chats with her mom about the exciting things she will do at school. Her mom tells her that school will be fun.

At school, there will be a hook with your name where you can hang your coat.

Shoes with Velcro can be easier than those with laces and buckles.

Veronika has been practicing putting on her shoes and coat.

Magic!

"Can you write your name?"

Adam likes to practice writing his name. He's found lots of fun ways to do it.

In the sand...

...with some chalk...

...and using modeling clay.

Tino

"I can use the toilet all by myself!"

When you use the toilet, make sure you wipe yourself clean with toilet paper afterward. Then, flush the toilet and wash and dry your hands.

I CAN... WASH MY HANDS

1. Wet your hands with water.
2. Squirt on some soap.
3. Rub the soapy water all around, in between your fingers, front and back. Do this for as long as it takes to sing the song "Happy Birthday" twice!
4. Rinse off the soap.
5. Dry your hands.

Getting ready

The big day is nearly here! Farah cannot wait to start school. Her parents help her to get ready. Here are some things that may help you, too.

Lay your clothes out the night before, so they are all ready to put on in the morning.

Uniform

Farah's mom has put a name tag in all her school clothes and shoes. It's a good idea because the children will have the same uniform, so clothes can easily get mixed up.

I love oatmeal and toast! My friend Isaac eats his breakfast at school.

Breakfast time

Eating breakfast gives you plenty of energy to start the day.

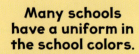

Many schools have a uniform in the school colors.

Things to take

Farah loves her reusable water bottle. Her dad has used a special kind of tape to put her name on it!

Farah takes a packed lunch to school in her lunch bag.

I CAN... BRUSH MY TEETH

1. Put a little toothpaste on your brush, and wet it.
2. Brush the fronts and insides of all your teeth in small circles.
3. Brush backward and forward on the chewing parts of your teeth.
4. Brush your tongue.
5. Spit out after brushing.

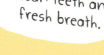

It feels good to go to school with clean teeth and fresh breath.

Smile!

Don't forget to have a photo of you looking excited for your first day. It's nice to show relatives and friends.

School bus

On the way

It's important to stay safe on the way to and from school. Look at the different ways the children who will be in Miss Smiley's class get to school.

Getting the bus
Some children travel on a school bus and others are driven in a car. Seat belts and car seats help us keep safe in vehicles.

Always cross at a safe place and hold an adult's hand.

Make sure to look and listen both ways before you cross the road.

Crossing

How do you get to school? Do you travel in a bus or car, or do you walk?

Crossing safely
A crossing guard stops the traffic so the children can cross the road safely.

The first day

Starting school is a big day for the children in Miss Smiley's class. They feel different things as they walk through the school gates. How do you feel about starting school?

Do you feel excited, shy, happy, confused, nervous, or something else?

I remember my first day here.

I am **excited**. I can't wait to make new friends and learn new things.

I feel **shy** about meeting new people. I'm glad my daddy is with me.

Anri

Niko

Does your new school look as big as this?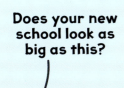

Adam holds onto his caretaker's hand tightly as he does not know where to go. Adam's caretaker has told him not to **worry** as she will go inside with him.

I CAN... MAKE A FEELINGS WHEEL

Ask an adult to draw a circle split into five parts, with a face in each part to show a different feeling. Use your wheel to talk about how you feel about starting school.

Libby feels **confused** as it's all so different from home.

Nathan is bursting with **happiness**. He loves playing outside and can't wait to run around the playground.

In the classroom

Look! Miss Smiley is waiting to say hello to her new class as they arrive. Their parents and caretakers can go inside with them on their first day. Niko feels braver already.

Coat pegs

Adam's caretaker shows him his peg where he will hang his coat. Adam is glad he has learned to read his name, as it helps him to find his peg.

I CAN... SPOT MY NAME

What things can you spot your name on? Can you see it on the labels on your school bag, and on your water bottle? Can you make the shape of the letter your name begins with in the air with your finger?

Today's school lunch menu

- Chicken and rice — NATHAN, JAMAL, AISHA
- Macaroni and cheese — TOM, TINO, VERONIKA, ANRI, RAFAEL
- Baked potato with toppings — ADAM, ZARA
- Packed lunch — MEG, ANGELO, CIARA, CHENG, LIBBY

What's for lunch?
The children choose their lunch from the school's menu in the morning. The pictures show lunch for today.

Rafael loves macaroni and cheese so he puts his name next to that.

Some children bring a packed lunch into school from home. What would you bring?

Circle time
The children are quiet on the carpet so they can hear when Miss Smiley calls out their name.

Good morning, Zara.

Good morning, Miss Smiley.

Tom raises his hand to ask a question.

Our schedule

This shows what Miss Smiley's class might do in a day. They have lessons, as well as times when they can choose what to do.

Morning

Literacy
This is about using letters and words. Rafael guesses which picture begins with an "ssss" sound.

Farah is good at writing the letter her name begins with.

Discovery time
Everyone can choose what to play with and discover new things together.

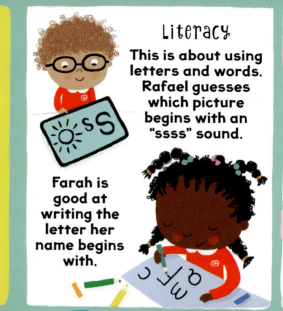

Lunch

Afternoon

"A snake can hiss. The word "hiss" ends in "ss"!"

Phonics
This is learning about letters and sounds.

Discovery time
The children can choose to do things inside or outside.

Cleanup time

cleanup time

snack time

Everyone has a drink and chooses a healthy snack.

outside time

The children run around outside in the fresh air.

Numbers
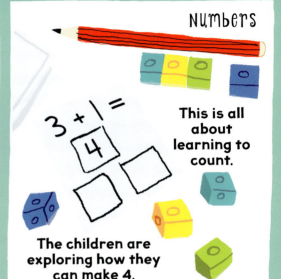
This is all about learning to count.

The children are exploring how they can make 4.

time

story time
It's good to calm down after a busy day before we go home.

pickup time

It's time to meet parents and caretakers.

I CAN... GET EXCITED!
Think about what you most look forward to doing at school. You could look through this book to help you decide. What do you like about it?

Settling in

Miss Smiley shows the children around their classroom. There are so many interesting things to do. Jamal thinks it will take him a while to remember where everything is!

Ask me or our teaching assistant Mrs. Latif if you forget where something is.

I have my own drawer for my things!

drawers

Art area

sensory table

What things can Niko see, hear, smell, and touch on the sensory table?

Splashing around

Ciara and Cheng are pouring water through funnels to see where it goes.

In the sand

Jasmine and Zara are pretending they are at the beach! Have you been to the beach? What would you like to do there?

Responsibility
I will look after my own things and try to work things out for myself first, when it's safe to do so.

Respect
I will be polite to others and help to keep the classroom tidy.

Our values

Miss Smiley wants everyone to feel happy and welcome in her class. Together, they talk about the school's values, which show them how they should try to behave.

If another child looks sad, give them a smile. It will help them to feel a bit better.

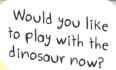

Would you like to play with the dinosaur now?

Fairness
I will take turns with things, and sometimes let others go first.

Responsibility
Respect
Fairness
Excellence
Kindness
Peace
Honesty

Excellence
I will try my best with everything I do.

I CAN... CALM DOWN

If you get mad or upset about something, calm down with some star breathing. Draw a big star on paper. Trace your finger up and down the sides of the star, breathing in each time you go up a side, and out when you go down a side. Keep doing it until you feel calm.

Star breathing

Sorry!

Kindness
I will listen to others and help others when they need it, if I can.

Peace
I will keep calm and will not shout or lose my temper.

Honesty
I will be brave enough to tell the truth, especially when I make a mistake.

Around the school

The school is a big place and there are lots of other rooms besides Miss Smiley's classroom. Miss Smiley takes the children around and shows them other parts of the school.

Hello, Himmat and Isaac. How do you like your new school?

The people who work in the **office** know everything that happens in school and all the students. They also help parents and caretakers with any questions they may have.

The children meet the **principal**, Mr. Bright. He has a very big job—he looks after the whole school!

We love it!

I CAN... DISCOVER NEW THINGS

Ask an adult to take you to a library and find a book on something new. Ask them to read it to you. Tell a friend something new you have learned.

The **Quiet Room** is a peaceful spot sometimes used by children instead of the classroom.

"I like coming here. It's a safe space for me to feel calm."

The janitor helps to keep the school clean and fixes things if they are broken.

Making friends

Some of the children find it easy to make new friends and others don't. Some have friends that are noisy and others that are quiet. Some friends might be a bit bossy and others can be shy.

Do you have any pets?

My name's Jamal. What are your names?

I'm Adam.

I'm Libby.

Questions
Think of two or three questions you could ask other children when you talk to them.

Things in common
Jamal likes building things and has made two new friends who enjoy building things too.

If someone is a bit shy you could ask them to join in with you.

Some of the children are playing together in the kitchen area. It's fun to pretend to make lunch!

New games
Farah asks Meg if she wants to join in the clapping game.

I haven't played this game before.

We'll show you.

Taking turns
Sofia and Rosie are outside. They take turns to ride on the blue scooter.

Lunchtime

Before Miss Smiley's class goes to lunch, they wash their hands. Then they are taken to the cafeteria. Each child having a school lunch wears a colored wristband to show the food they have chosen.

A helping hand
As well as lunchtime helpers, older children from the school help out on the first few days.

You're having macaroni and cheese, Rafael.

Thank you!

Some children bring a packed lunch with them.

What did I pick?
Rafael has forgotten the food he chose for today. The lunchtime helper reminds him.

If you see someone on their own, it's kind to ask them if they would like to sit with you.

It's loud
Some people like noise and some don't. Tino finds the cafeteria noisy. He wears headphones so it's not so loud.

Recycling
It helps our planet if we recycle our trash. Plastic can be made into other things and food can be turned into compost.

"Aisha, would you like to sit with us?"

"Yes please."

I CAN... MAKE A HEALTHY SNACK POT

Make a fruit or vegetable snack pot. Wash a container, such as a yogurt container. Choose your snacks and ask an adult to chop them. Wash and arrange in the pot, and add some dip if you like. Enjoy!

What will we learn?

This month, Miss Smiley's class is finding out all about the sea and the animals that live in it. Adam has discovered that dolphins talk to each other in clicks and whistles.

Shipwreck!
The home corner has been turned into a shipwreck and the children have found treasure! What treasure have they found?

I'm making the clicking noises dolphins make.

Castanets

Drum

This sounds like waves on a sandy beach.

Sea sounds
Adam and Ciara make sounds that remind them of the sea.

Sink or float?

Sofia and Rosie are finding and sorting things that float and sink. Can you guess if the plastic rings will float or sink?

Sea creatures

Look at the super underwater picture Jamal is painting. Can you see the octopus?

"Sea" begins with an "ssss" sound, and the letter looks like a curly snake.

Learning letters

Everyone learns in different ways. Isaac gets extra help with his writing.

The end of the day

After a busy first day, it's time to clean up and then sit quietly on the carpet to listen to a story before going home. Miss Smiley reads a story about a fish, which fits in with their sea topic.

A helper signs the words so Meg, who is deaf, can enjoy the story too.

Frida thought she had the most beautiful, shiny scales in all the sea.

I CAN... INVENT A CHARACTER

Invent a character for a story. Give them a name, draw a picture of them, and make up an adventure for them to go on. Tell your story to a friend or your teacher.

Time to go home

After the story, a few children at a time collect their coats and book bags. Then everybody lines up to go home. It takes a while for them all to get ready!

Looking at a book is a great way to relax after a fun day.

Book bags

Each child is given a book bag to take books home in. Zara can't wait to look inside. Her bag has a bookmark and a reading record so her parents can write notes to the teacher.

"I can't wait to look at this book with my daddy."

After school

Miss Smiley knows who is picking up every child. The children make sure they know who is picking them up too. Libby's babysitter will look after her until her dad picks her up later.

My day
Libby can't wait to tell her babysitter all about her first day at school.

Cheng and Veronika play snakes and ladders.

Niko, Isaac, and Anri make things on the craft table.

After-school club
Some of the children go straight to the cafeteria for after-school club. There are lots of activities to try. What have they chosen?

Letting off steam

As soon as Nathan gets home, he grabs his bike and rushes out into the yard to ride around.

Tell your family, or even your pet if you have one, all about your day at school.

What do you like to do when you get home?

I CAN... MAKE A FORT

Make a fort to relax in after school. Put some chairs back-to-back with space in between for your fort. Then hang a large sheet or blanket over them. Put some blankets inside, and ask an adult to hang some fairy lights.

Playdate

Rosie's friend Sofia has come over to play. They love playing with Rosie's dog, Charlie.

The first week

With each new day, the children get to know what they like doing. They look forward to their favorite things, and enjoy trying some exciting new activities.

Can you spot a tambourine?

Music
Jamal loves singing and clapping to the beat while Mrs. Bell, the music teacher, plays her guitar and sings.

That's all the sugar we need, Maddy.

Cooking
The children are making snack bars. Yum! Miss Smiley helps Tom tip the oats into the mixing bowl.

Oats
Syrup
Sugar

Junk modeling

The children had an amazing afternoon cutting, sticking, and fixing boxes and tubes together! Anri is proud of her model. Can you guess what she has made?

Make your own junk dragon out of boxes, glue, and card stock.

Gardening

There are some vegetable beds outside. The children learn that plants need soil, water, and sunlight to grow.

The seeds Jasmine has planted are growing into pea plants!

Butter

"I'm waiting until it's my turn to walk along the bench."

Mixing it up
The children try different ways of moving. They go **on** things, **under** things, **around** things, and **through** things.

High bench

Low bench

All bodies are different. We are all good at different things and may need extra help sometimes.

"We have changed into loose clothes and sneakers so it is easier to move around."

Mat

Cone

Get moving
Being active helps our bodies and minds stay healthy and happy. Anri is so excited as her class is having their first gym class.

Putting on a play

Sometimes the children put on a play in the hall. The whole school and families come to watch.

Stage

At the end, everyone comes on stage to take a bow.

In the hall

Many events happen in the big hall. It is often a place for sharing. Today Miss Smiley's class join the other classes for an assembly.

Celebrating

Mr. Bright gives some of the children in Miss Smiley's class stickers for their good manners. They feel very proud.

Well done, Tom, for being kind.

Thank you, Mr. Bright.

Singing

Mrs. Bell tells the children to look up and imagine they are singing out loud to an audience.

Singing can make you feel happy – especially if you sing in a group with friends.

Showing our work

Some of the class goes to the front to show the work they have been doing to the other children.

The rest of the children sit quietly on the floor in rows.

I CAN... MAKE LEAF-PRINTED BUGS

Paint underneath some leaves, then press the leaves onto paper to make leaf prints. When they are dry, add faces and legs to turn them into beautiful bugs.

Meg loves feeling the cold mud squish and squelch in the mud hole.

Mud hole

Mud Painting

Cheng is enjoying painting patterns on a tree trunk with mud.

Zara feels brave getting on the wobbly seesaw.

Adam thinks he might try it out next time.

Bug hotel

Aisha and Isaac are proud of the home they have made for bugs. They have used things with lots of holes for the bugs to hide in.

"We have filled it with things bugs love to eat!"

"They build nests in it too."

Wonderful writing

Before the children start writing words, they get used to making patterns and shapes. Take a piece of paper and try copying these patterns. They go up and down, across, and around.

Tip 1: Try writing with chunky crayons and pencils, mini pencils, or a paintbrush.

Tip 2: Trace the patterns in the air or on the page with your finger.

Tip 3: Trace the patterns in sand with a stick or the end of a wooden spoon.

Here are some fun things the children do that will help them with holding a pencil. Try them for yourself.

Can you think of some other things you do with your hands?

1. Coloring in

2. Pouring

3. Twisting and opening lids

Some children find it easier to use their left hand and some find things easier with their right hand.

4. Shaping modeling clay

45

Nifty numbers

The children have made up a rhyme to help them remember the order of numbers from one to ten. What counting rhymes do you know?

"One, two, a cow goes moo."

Can you make up a counting rhyme?

"Three, four, jam on the floor."

"Five, six, try some new tricks."

Jasmine loves to whiz around on her bike.

"Seven, eight, I am late."

"Nine, ten, let's sing it again!"

Can you find?

Look back through the pages of this book to find the answers to these questions.

Let's find out together!

1. What is the name of the special set of clothes for Farah on page 8?
2. Will Adam hang his coat in a cupboard or on a hook on page 14?
3. What does the schedule say will happen just before pickup time on page 17?
4. What are Maddy and Sofia doing on page 19?
5. How many children are playing on the tricycles on pages 20–21?
6. Who is holding a broom on page 25?
7. What instrument is Ciara playing on page 30?
8. What animal is Zara's book about on page 33?
9. What is Nathan wearing to protect his head on page 35?
10. What does Mr. Bright give to Tom on page 40?

You can check your answers here!

ANSWERS
1. Uniform
2. A hook
3. Story time
4. Reading
5. Four
6. The janitor
7. A drum
8. A lion
9. A helmet
10. A sticker